A Gaggle of Verses

VONNA ADRIAN

a gaggle of verses

Bits Press
Cleveland

Printed and bound in the U.S.A.
ISBN: 0-933248-09-1.

CONTENTS

TELL ME, JULIA

" . . . Julia's dainty Leg,
Which is as white and hairless as an egge."
— Robert Herrick

Tell me, Julia, you glittering girl
with the glow-worm eyes,
you silken study in liquefaction:

Did your sweetly flowing silks
kindle an wantonness?
Did you lose control
of a tempestuous petticoat?
Did you aim at this exhibit
to tickle a cleric's eye?

Or did his eggy simile
originate, as some have said,
only in his head?

GEORGE I

A Matter of Taste

Suppose a monarch's graced with style:
A touch of guile
or tyranny, so Tories owned,
might be condoned.

But *that* one now, that German boor
with a paramour
so ponderous that even Whigs
took sly digs
at her — he scorned a meager waist
as a matter of taste.

How crude of him, implying a slight
to pert Nell Gwynn
and her willing kin
who reigned when light-o-loves were light!

GEORGE II

At the Haymarket Theatre

Majestic paeans to the *King*
of Kings and Lord of Lords! Ecstatic,
they roused the lesser king. Phlegmatic,
portly, he rose in the royal box.

Was he in tune with art, or faith,
that Handel had such power to budge him?
Or did his Consort lean and nudge him
to rise and set a precedent?

No matter. He ennobled for us
the immortal Hallalujah Chorus.

GEORGE III

At Weymouth

> "When the King splashed into the sea from his royal [bathing] machine, he was followed by another machine in which a small congested orchestra played the National Anthem."
>
> — C. E. Vulliamy, *Royal George*

The Royal Porpoise,
clad in modest azure serge,
plunges and plashes to submerge
his kingly corpus
in the Dorset main
to a loyal strain.

Britannia's Darling,
he rules the waves at Weymouth beach,
and when he hears the band beseech
"God Save the King,"
he stands offshore
for an encore.

GEORGE IV

His Coronation

> "Caroline drove up to the Abbey and at every door was turned away. "Your ticket," they asked her. "I have none, and as Queen of England I need none."
>
> — Geoffrey Dennis,
> *Coronation Commentary*

His Queen arrived in an open-topped carriage
to see him annointed.
She left disappointed,
cursing the man, cursing the marriage,
berating them shrilly
all through Piccadilly.

With ambassadors, prelates, and nobles invited
to convene in the Abbey,
wasn't it shabby
for the Queen to be so brutally slighted?
Demanding her ticket
was hardly cricket.

JONATHAN SWIFT, DEAN OF ST. PATRICK'S

Dublin's dean, though keen
to rise, remained a dean.

Duller and politer,
he might have worn a mitre.

DR. JOHNSON'S AFTERNOON

A snuff-brown whale rolled with the tide
of London herring through Fleet and Strand,
wallowing blind in his own gloom.
"Sir, your pardon," when he'd collide
with any who swam that narrow flume.
He surfaced at the Mitre, planned
to spout awhile and override
a fragile fin or two (poor Nolly!)*
then when day and night converged,
roll back home and lie submerged
in tea, and prayer, and melancholy.

*Oliver Goldsmith

TO MRS. MONTAGU, BLUESTOCKING AT EIGHTEEN

"Contemplation is not made for a woman on the right side of thirty."

— Elizabeth Robinson Montagu,
"Queen of the Blues"

Dear Mrs. Montagu,
you pretty kitten you,
eighteen is nowhere near the wrong side.
How then, how could you
so early join that blue
coterie, that crew
with brains so plainly on the strong side,
charms so strongly on the plain side?
Lovely Montagu,
you might have lingered on the vain side.
Dear Mrs. Montagu,
why didn't you?

WILLIAM BLAKE ENTERTAINS

Master Blake was a genial host
when Mary Wollstonecraft came calling,
or John Milton, or the Holy Ghost,
or Crabb Robinson, or the Queen
of Heaven, or Michelangelo —
whoever traveled down the green
lane to his cottage door.
                                        Enthralling,
their talk: a blend of Long Ago
with Time-to-Come and Here-and-Now.
His eye kindled; his hearkening brow
held communion. The after glow
still lingered on while he held them
in turn with a rare portfolio
of plans for the New Jerusalem.

WALTER, THAT SAVAGE LANDOR

Nature he loved, in verse he said it,
and yet to his discredit
he hurled the cook into the garden.

True, he begged Dame Nature's pardon,
Clasping his white impetuous head:
"God! I forgot the violet bed!"

ROBERT SOUTHEY AT HOME

"Southey was intemperately fond of black currant rum."

— Ernest Bernbaum

His worldly goods endowed his bride,
  and snug was Edith Fricker.
But when he'd barely settled down,
  or maybe even quicker,
came Widow Lovell, destitute —
  Lovell, *née* Mary Fricker —
begging harbor for self and child.
  (One pardons him a flicker
of apprehension.) Coleridge too,
  and wife, *née* Sara Fricker,
devoured his bounty, as now and then
  with querulous female bicker,
did Martha and Eliza, the two
  penniless Misses Fricker.

Rumor claims he never spoke
  a word to shock a vicar;
rumor also claims he sipped
  a potent currant liquor
and swam in Lethe far from shore,
  far from the House of Fricker.

A MOMENT IN DOVE COTTAGE

"Oh, the darling! Here is one of his bitten apples."

— Dorothy Wordsworth's *Grasmere Journal*

Nowhere else in all of Britain
was sister so with brother smitten.
With due regard to whose dental
imprint the apple bore, her gentle
cooing seems excessive. Fitter
to toss the object out with litter
and utter with housewifely vim,
"Ugh! How untidy of him!"

TO DOROTHY WORDSWORTH, WITH LOVE

Your *Journal*'s a rosary of hours
strung on a four-ply cord.
  Beads of clay
    with pearls between,
  they glide away.

Finger the beads of sober clay:
William's mended coat,
  radishes hoed,
    firewood gathered,
  the spinach sowed,

linens laid on the grass to bleach,
the oven-fragrant bread,
  newspapers filed,
    the carpet bound,
  red apples piled.

Finger the beads of lucent pearl:
hepatica under snow,
  mist on the lake,
    a thrush in the orchard,
  fern in the brake,

a crescent hanging moon above
black crags, strawberry bloom
  springing wild,
    white woolly lambs
  April beguiled.

These are your hours that glide along
the four-ply cord — four strands
  in a twist of pain:
    Coleridge, William,
  headache, and rain.

MARTIN FARQUHAR TUPPER, PHILOSOPHER

What levity he sparked, he never guessed.
Good owl, he prophesied as he was able —
obvious matter in lofty phrase. But best
of all — and this gave cause for him to preen
his owl plumage — he gratified his Queen,
who kept his opus* on her parlor table.

**Proverbial Philosophy*, 1857

VICTORIA REGINA FIRMA

Tobacco, Women's Rights,
The Prince of Wales, divorce —
on all, her views lay fixed
like cubes of fruit in the firm
aspic of her mind.

She held that territory
through quakes and queries fit
to topple a palace wall.
None woke the slightest jiggle
in the royal jelly mold.

MR. AND MRS. BROWNING

After the Séance

Plainly Mr. B.
is out of sympathy.
How could Ba succumb
to a canting medium?
He dare not utter "Scum!"
or "Fraud!" or "Pabulum!"

Connubial harmony
recommends that he
not flout the brave Miss Ba
who flouted her papa.
Thus his anathema
fades to a feeble "Pshaw!"
and Ba is spared a "Bah!"

TENNYSON AND BROWNING, *SARTUS*

The flowing locks, the crumpled cape,
the battered sable wide-awake,
all worn with negligence and ease:
this was the image Alfred T.
affected. In truth, it was no pose —
he merely clung to his old clothes.

Such a get-up Robert B.
deplored as pseudo-poetic weeds.
He served as model for his own
sartorial policy: to go
barbered and suited like any clerk
on a Sunday stroll through Regent's Park.

AN AFTERNOON AT FARRINGFORD

"Emily took basket exercise today."

— Alfred Lord Tennyson

The day is fine, and Lady T.
forsakes her sofa for the nonce
to take the air in her *pleasaunce.*
Under the cedars go the three:
shaggy pony, poet, and she.

Poet leads pony, and pony draws
basket with lady. (The bit in his jaws
pinches; he longs for a ration of hay
and a roll on the downs at close of day.)

They turn back now in time for tea,
poet and pony and chatelaine
well aired and exercised, with gain
in muscle tone for two of the three,
not paired by license in Chancery.

A PAIR OF WORTHIES

> "Do thou help me, my little woman;
> thou art worthy of that destiny."
>
> — letter of Thomas Carlyle to Jane

She valued this encomium
from one who was, though rather glum,
a genius. How did she gauge
the merit of her Chelsea sage?

By judging him worthy of his Jane —
testimonial to the brain
lighting her cranium, because,
of course, her Thomas almost was.

EXIT KATE DICKENS, JUNE 1858

"The little pill-box on wheels that staggers about London with Mrs. Dickens."

— Letter of Charles Dickens to
Leigh Hunt

She's signed her name, agreed to terms.
A legal contract now confirms
her as a bungler in her marriage,
discarded, pitied, and derided.
It leaves her nevertheless provided
with status: one who "keeps her carriage"
now drives away from the family scene,
tying her bonnet strings between
those more than ample twins —
her trembling double chins.

SWINBURNE'S LAST YEARS

The flame dwindles, the frenzy passes.
He strolls uphill to The Green Man
to take his frugal daily tankard.
He'll not dare the steeper path
that leads from Putney to Parnassus.

DANTE GABRIEL ROSSETTI

Weary, willowy damozels
with slumbrous gaze
and languid ways
thronged his canvases,
glided through his dreams.
  But Fanny was a doxy —*
  ah, cry paradox!

Fanny was a hussy,
florid and obese,
a hearty, greedy, fussy,
unmysterious piece.
She screamed with Cockney mirth,
this ever human, nosy,
carnal daughter of earth.
In short, the wench was prosy
rather than poetic. Yet he
pillowed on her charms
for twenty years; Rossetti
reveled in her round warm arms.

Weary, willowy damozels,
ethereal, sybilline,

*Fanny Cornforth, mistress and occasional model

of mystic mien,
thronged his canvases,
glided through his dreams.
  But Fanny was a doxy —
  ah, cry paradox!

CHRISTINA ROSSETTI AT EVENSONG

"Christina, your heart may be like a singing bird, but why do you dress like a pew opener?"

— D. G. Rossetti, according to Max Beerbohm.

Christina tried to pay no heed
to brotherly and brutal taunting.
Christina tried to quell her need
for a whisper of silken flounces flaunting
down a London High Church aisle.
In dowdy bonnet she knelt, and knew
how momentary the somber while
here below till her bright debut
on high!
Oh beatific vision,
Oh stately Anglican soirée,
her self denial's sweet fruition!
Of all the sainted, none soignée
as she adorns the esplanade
of Heaven. Pre-Raphaelite, enwrought
with fleur-de-lis, her white brocade
ripples in jeweled panels shot
with gold. And all the incorporeal
host, with clergy here and there
agape, salute her bright sartorial
spirit ascending a Burne-Jones stair.

MARIA FRANCESCA ROSSETTI

In the British Museum

Sister Maria's eyeballs bulge
with a thought appalling to divulge:
What if, *what if* the Day of Doom
falls now to free the saint, devour
the sinner? (Ye know not the hour.)
What if — she here in the mummy room —
the sleeping bones should wake and rend
their linen wrappings, crack their cases,
put on flesh with holy grimaces?
How could she watch that host ascend
on swooping wing, chanting *Te Deum*
above the dome of the British Museum?
How stand rooted with vulgar stare,
an outrage to High Church decorum,
waiting her turn for the Judgment Forum?

Out through the gate, to Russell Square
and beyond, trots Sister Maria, fleeing
ill breeding — safe for the time being.

WEDDING AT ST. GEORGE'S, HANOVER SQUARE

At quarter past ten, Thursday, 6 May, 1880, Miss Mary Ann Evans [George Eliot] to John Walter Cross, Esquire.

— *The Times*

Exeunt from the portico a pair:
the youthful bridegroom dapper as D'Orsay,
the bride mature and somewhat horsy.
Whether she wears what maidens wear,

or garb more seemly, to say the least,
whether a veil, or plumes, or prim bow,
the record lurks, alas, in limbo
along with the name of her modiste.

No matter; one thing's certain — this is
our sybil lapsed to a legal Mrs.

TO HETTY SORREL

Reprieved at the Gallows Foot

Pretty Hetty, Hetty Sorrel,
were you proud to point a moral
warning all the shire's rural
maids to turn from mortal sin
and shun the pickle you were in?
Proud to think the lesson learnt?
No, I guess you weren't.

Pretty Hetty, Hetty Sorrel,
unconcerned to point a moral,
were you grateful in your peril,
feeling your stony heart stirred
to know the kindly court preferred
to see you gently hanged, not burnt?
No, I guess you weren't.

PHRASES TOWARD A SENTENCE DEFINING HENRY JAMES'S PREFERENCES IN FEMALE COMPANIONSHIP

No truelove to escort,
or mistress to support,
or wife to cherish — in short,

no bond with womankind
but, as it were, confined
to dalliance with her mind,

to, if you will, a chronic
caution lest a cyclonic
urge — term it Byronic —

should lead to, might one say
a path, or rather *allée?*
of peril, yea or nay,

his *nay* to be counted on,
a mark of libido gone,
or going, a phenomenon,

a thread — more apt, a cord —
tugging him to, or toward,
Mrs. Humphrey Ward . . .

YEATS AND HORTICULTURE

"Nine bean rows"? Merely a topic
for verse. Never could those myopic
eyes tell a bean from a honeybee!

Not so his Georgie — for it was she
who tilled and tended that Galway rose
the poet, keen for a symbol, chose.

A CLUTCH OF CLERIHEWS

St. Jerome
abandoned brush and comb
and bread and jam and everything nice.
He did it on divine advice.

St. Simeon Stylites
was Lord Almighty's
problem child. He mounted a pillar and overstayed
waiting for heaven's accolade.

Mary Tudor
was maybe bloodier and ruder
than her pa to traitors and such —
but not much.

Geoffrey Chaucer
never drank from a cup and saucer,
but that's no cause for mockery;
he lived before the age of genteel crockery.

Miss Elizabeth Barrett
didn't care at
all when Wimpole Street was chill and foggy;
she lounged indoors with a little doggy.

Alfred Lord Tennyson
preferred his venison
left on the hoof, but like a glutton,
denied this clemency to mutton.

William Butler Yeats
on alternating dates
could extol a bawd
and moon over Maud.

A PLAGUEY THING

If I were you I'd just forget it;
a pantoum is a plaguey thing.
It drives you crazy if you let it;
it haunts you, day and evening.

A pantoum is a plaguey thing.
My friend, can you define *pantoum*?
It haunts you day and evening;
does it belong in a drawing room?

My friend, can you define *pantoum*?
Do you strum it, or pluck it, or beat it?
Does it belong in a drawing room?
If fruit or veg, then you could eat it.

Do you strum it, or pluck it, or beat it?
Dare mail it to a little mag?
If fruit or veg, then you could eat it.
Producing it can be a drag.

Dare mail it to a little mag,
it drives you crazy if you let it.
Producing it can be a drag.
If I were you I'd just forget it.

CALL US POETESSES

We are the lady poets. We
dote on delicate terms for things:
Our birds never fly on prosy wings,
but cleave the ether on radiant pinions.
We are the lady poets, minions
of a muse unerringly genteel,
and yet we're fired by a holy zeal
and often, often, soar aloft.
I mean to say, we do it oft.
Our meter's an almost perfect canter.
(*Almost*? "Well nigh" sounds eleganter.)
We stab you with signs of exclamation,
thus rousing feeling through punctuation.

Ah yes, we are the lady poets.
Who rates our talent as itty-bitty?
Come now, admit it, our poems are pretty!!!

LITERARY CLUB, OLD STYLE

A poet's come from out of town
to read his work. Some members glow
to indicate they're in the know;
some members look intent and frown,
while others watch the kitchen door
and calculate how long the bore
has yet to go.
                    At last, at last,
oh lyric moment! A frozen sonnet
with butterscotch and almonds on it!

AUTRES TEMPS, AUTRES MOEURS

"When the ladies left the table, someone spoke of Shakespeare."

— R. C. Lehman, *Memories of Half a Century*

Someone was a gentleman.
Spooning his green turtle broth,
Someone deftly captivated
his left-hand lady with verbal froth.
Launching no Oxonian
prattle of Goth and Visigoth,
Voltaire, Burne-Jones, or Kublai Khan,
Someone kept his small talk small:
the Derby, or the latest troth,
Milady's eyes, a costume ball.
Yet all the while he estimated
the hour old port would replace the cloth
and taffeta be segregated.
But how the hostess lagged, how wroth
he grew till at last, "Gad! Free men!"
And Someone spoke of Shakespeare then.

I SUPPOSE I COULD LOOK IT UP

He's studying etymology —
or is it entomology?
Which one's all about words,
Which about bugs — or is it birds?

INEVITABLE

A piglet's cuddlesome and plump;
how pinchable a piglet's rump!
A piglet's charming, clean, and cute,
a winsome creature, tail to snoot —

till time and fate conspire somehow
to change our piglet into sow.

'TIS THE VOICE OF THE SLUGGARD

Ant, you're whistle clean
in glossy black, but you've got
no play suit. Why so keen
on hoisting burdens a lot
too big for you? You irk
me by your motto, *Work*
For Night Is Coming When Ant
Will Work No More. How smug,
how preachy, how irritant
you are to a genial bug
who'd rather not be wise!
Go to the sluggard, thou ant,
go and apologize.

BIBLE STORY HOUR

"A good man — Abraham," my grandma said.
She pointed out a picture: robed in red
he loomed on the sky, and keen-honed terror flashed
in his right hand. "Bad man!" I cried, and pushed
the story book aside. The *thud-a-thud-*
a-thud of Isaac's heart, the tingling blood
of the bleating lamb, echoed in my own.
The smart of smoke, the altar's jagged stone
under the naked thighs, the cruel taut thong
on straining flesh, I knew. But I judged wrong,
my grandma said, for "This was just the way
Jehovah took to learn if he'd obey."
"Jehovah? Who was he?" "The same as God,"
she said. But I could not accept this libel,
for God was good. I knew that he was good
better than Grandma did, or Holy Bible.

ROLL CALL IN EDEN

> "And whatever Adam called every living creature, that was the name thereof."
>
> — Genesis 2:19

Lord God bade Adam call, call,
call every creature by its name.
Lion, Leopard, Lamb,
circling round the Tree they came;
up from Tigris swam
Crocodile to hear his name.

They frolicked round the fruited Tree
and Leopard nuzzled Lamb. The plush
of Tiger's striped flank
met Zebra's there . . . until a hush
chilled the circling rank,
chilled the bloom on vine and bush:

Serpent! rang the call, call,
Serpent! Through the shuddering leaves
slid Serpent, smiling to foresee
red rage in Rhino's eye, and fall
of blood on emerald grass
beneath the ruby-fruited Tree.

BRIDE IN EDEN

When Adam's rib arose and stood
  beside her dreaming lord, the doe
  peered from the leaves, mild eyes aglow
to welcome kin of gentle blood.

But vixen and tigress, circling, knew
in Adam's bride a sister, too.

RUN, SWEET PANTHER

> THE PANTHER is not only handsome but very kind. Among the animals it counts only the dragon its enemy. A lovely ringing sound comes from its mouth, together with a delightful smell of blossoms and herbs, like allspice. The animals of the forest follow the panther because of the fragrance of its breath. Only the dragon flees the panther.
>
> — Medieval bestiary

Run, sweet panther, race
the fleeing dragon (spawn
of serpent, he, guilty
of guile since Adam's bride).
Sweet panther, overtake
The Enemy, with song
and allspice vanquish him.
Not St. George's way:
kill dragon-sire, inflame
his kin. No, breathe song
and allspice, then shall he
beam benignity,
flame-flickering tongue
lolling, cooled by kindness.
Run, sweet panther! Run!

IN A HOSPITAL NURSERY

The plate-glass barrier muffled sound,
but not the flooding tide of red
anguish that your wailing spread
across your petal face. You frowned

and tensed yourself, your fist tight curled.
It was as if you only took
one filmy, out-of-focus look —
and judged ill weather ruled the world.

HOW SAD IS OUR LUNCHROOM NOW

Hey junky-jinky,
the kid and the Twinkie:

they met every noon
till our Miss Veggie

came by and hollered,
"How junky-jinky!

DOWN with the Twinkie,
UP with the carrot,

celery-elery,
Broccoli-occoli,

zucchini-ini,
parsnipity-ipity,

DOWN with the Twinkie,
hey junkie-jinky!"

A DOGGEREL PSALM OF LIFE

She stayed at home to keep the house
and nurse her pa with barley water.
His will enriched his other daughter.
  "That's life," we said.

He played the violin with hands
that granted us a glimpse of soul,
but when arthritis took its toll,
  "That's life," we said.

The Boy Most Likely to Succeed
perversely set himself to fail,
and when he hanged himself in jail,
  "That's life," we said.

She saved her cash and paid the fare
for a luxury cruise. Wouldn't you know —
she cracked her pelvis and couldn't go.
  "That's life," we said.

Clearly, the game's a lottery.
Why not go limp and give it up?
Why all this urge to live it up?
  "That's life," we say.

TORNADO

I'd never seen so queer a morning
on the prairie — breathless, still.
Our uncut wheatfield stood dead-ripe,
an amber block — as if a spell
had stopped its stirring.

I'd set a baking in the oven
(pies to feed the morrow's crew
of harvest hands), but when I stepped
outside again to rest, I knew
a shiver running

through the wheatfield's living gold.
You've seen the way the air before
a storm turns luminous? Our barn
glowed weirdly red; the sycamore,
fluorescent green.

Lime-yellow lit the zenith; purple
darkened all the west with wrath.
I read bleak ruin in the sky,
knew all we owned was in its path;
yet my despair

and terror warred with eerie beauty's
strange elation. Ample time
ahead for fear — storm-cellared fear,

I thought; but first: one last, sublime —
one last, long gaze!

I still recall how *light* I felt —
how glad no one was there to see
me, hear me lift my arms and sing
against the wind, exulting, free:
"Oh *glory*, GLORY!"

PRAIRIE CHURCH

White-painted, bare, rectangular,
it stands where prairie sun beats down,
bleaching the roof. The door's ajar;
come in and breathe the homely brown
scent of virtue that bespeaks
the Dorcas Ladies' ministry
of naphtha soap. The pulpit reeks
of recent varnish, a homily
in itself. And that frail balm
of June, gracing this rigorous air
with mercy, floating like a psalm
above the gilded Mason jar
of honeysuckle — clearly, this is
a golden text from "Reverend Mrs."
Come in and breathe the mingled three:
here is the odor of sanctity.

1925

THE WAY IT WAS ON MAPLE STREET

Gold and fire, the branches meet
over neighbors burning leaves,
burning leaves on Maple Street.

We lean on rakes to watch. The gift
from maple trees endows the blaze,
blessing it with golden drift.

It seems as if flame might aspire
to meet that fall of lambent fuel
in equilibrium of fire —

as once at Pentecost, when prayer
kindled and rose like flame to call
Godhead down in radiant power.

SUMMIT

Here from this granite height I trace my road
looping below. The day lingers. Sunset
colors the quiet river, tints the sheep
on the far hillside. Dark pines repeat the white
thrust of the village spire. How red the glow
of roof tile through the green of elm and larch!
How friendly the town where I could never tarry!
The altitude, the hour — how they reveal
the view, charting the road I had to find,
but never looked at, never knew till now.

LAST PHOTOGRAPH

"I was looking at that old photograph
the other day."

— Thomas Wolfe

That Sunday was a sun day, bleaching the last
of the blue asters along the galvanized
wire fence. You wore your uniform and posed
frowning, squinting square into the lens.
A yellow poplar leaf came floating home
to your left shoulder.
                                        Flooding sun that dimmed
your image on the film, fading the gold
insignia, descends with mercy now
where green falters back to bereaved boughs.

MEMORY

Dark pool,
deep pool of clouded water:
what heavy stones
plunge
to bruise
its muddy bed!

Dark pool,
deep pool where no sun
comes to probe
your words
to me
that day.

SALVATION ON SUNSET MOUNTAIN

Evangel Sun goes shouting down the west
to coral *hallelujahs*, amethyst
amen, amen re-echoing after him.
It's late, and I must leave the canyon rim
for the homeward trail. I hear a boulder go
bumpa-bump-bumping down the slope below:
so light I feel in the winey air, so light
to hear that boulder roll, that I could quite
believe it the burden Bunyan's Pilgrim shed
upon his saintly Progress. Unballasted
by sin I'll soar awhile, and then start down
through stunted pines. How soon will I admit
I'm half hoping to catch up with it
somewhere along the highway into town?

THERE

I was there once. Alone. Without a map.
It could have been the Cheviot hills, but wasn't.

I only know the air turned opal after
rain, and sheep drifted like snow along
the slope. The tender dialogue of ewes
and lambs swelled to an antiphonal chorale,
alto *baa-a* answered by treble *maa-a*.
I learned, or rather knew, the simple language
of the flock. I plunged my hands into their dense
rain-damp fleece. I met their recognizing
gaze and called each one by name — Gertrude,
Amy, Belinda, Molly, Miranda — we all
gossiped like sisters there on friendly grass.

Yes, I was there once. Will I ever find
Eden again in the far hills of sleep?

SOUVENIR

How young we were! How many Junes ago
did we first view the dunes along this shore?
Great swirling mounds — we gathered shells below
their shade. Tomorrow? That, we could ignore.

When we returned on yearly honeymoons
the landscape seemed eternal — like love, we said,
for happiness was stable as the dunes.
Last night, in balmy June, unheralded,

our frail retreat was lashed by hurricane.
Like youth and health, landscape can disappear!
We'll not return, but mind will still retain
our days upon the dunes — our souvenir.

Aware today of all that's fleeting, I'll
take heed and memorize my loved one's smile.

WINTER LOVE SONG

In the heart of winter, fleet
season of tangerines,
we aging lovers tarry,
dwindling with the year.

Now when the chills of flu
flutter my thermostat,
I wait for a tart-sweet fountain
to freshen my fevered tongue.

Winter's the time, my love,
for cherishing: you plump
my rumpled pillow, smooth
the blanket, relay the news,

bring aspirin and toast
and tea. (What young Juliet
so pampered by Romeo?)
You come now, old magician,

with a peeled tangerine.
Quick flick of thumbs — *presto,*
petals! O pungent rose
of winter love, unclose!

POSSESSION

Dearer than mate or child, the story goes,
great-grand-aunt Milly loved this house, and wept
to hear her brother named the heir. She chose
her course then, heedless of the family rift.

Time and again she came unheralded
as if to claim a right to view the rooms,
inspecting carpets, plumping a featherbed,
purging a vase of wilted aster blooms.

At midnight now, with wind lifting the white
curtains and twitching my heirloom counterpane,
I wake and tremble in the chill moonlight,
listening, waiting till it comes again:

that pale mist sighing along the window sill,
The house belongs to me, and always will.

FINAL ARCH

When she had entered on her final days
Aunt Ella said it was as if she walked
a long black tunnel toward a dazzling arch
of sky.

And we who quailed to watch her tread
the path of pain, saw how she never lost
the vista through that widening arch ahead.
It led her down the center, arrow-straight
through darkness, as in childlike faith she glimpsed
tomorrow as a sun-gilt meadow where
the sheep and Shepherd breathed eternal June.
Tomorrow? Aunt had always lived today.

So even then, in narrow dark and chill,
her questing fingers joyed in creviced ferns
and moss embroidering her tunnel walls.
She filled the cup of dying with the cool
sweet water from some spring she found along
her way.

And so we hardly could have known
the hour she gained the tunnel's final arch
and stood a moment in the threshold sun . . .
We hardly could have known the hour — had we
not seen that sun reflected in her eyes.

We drew the blinds that day (as custom bade),
but knew them drawn against a lesser sun.

HOME TO BETHLEHEM

I came to Bethlehem
at dusk, from walking down
the years. The stars all knelt
behind the hill; the town
lay lulled by a wrinkling breeze
through the silver olive trees.
Then where sky and hill
met, a star rose, chill
in the pale dusk — one star
to kindle myriads, till
they all rose caroling,
a blazing choir to sing
me home to Bethlehem.